Dear Ashlyn – To our
Readers

Praise for the Believe Series

"As grandparents of fifty grandchildren, we heartily endorse the *Believe and You're There* series. Parents and grandparents, gather your children around you and discover the scriptures again as they come alive in the *Believe and You're There* series."

—STEPHEN AND SANDRA COVEY
Stephen Covey is the bestselling author of *7 Habits of Highly Effective People*

"Bravo! This series is a treasure! You pray that your children will fall in love with and get lost in the scriptures just as they are discovering the wonder of reading. This series does it. Two thumbs way, way up!"

—MACK AND REBECCA WILBERG
Mack Wilberg is the music director of the Mormon Tabernacle Choir

"This series is a powerful tool for helping children learn to liken the scriptures to themselves. Helping children experience the scriptural stories from their point of view is genius."

—ED AND PATRICIA PINEGAR
Ed Pinegar is the bestselling author of *Raising the Bar*

"We only wish these wonderful books had been available when we were raising our own children. How we look forward to sharing them with all our grandchildren!"

—STEPHEN AND JANET ROBINSON
Stephen Robinson is the bestselling author of *Believing Christ*

"The *Believe and You're There* series taps into the popular genre of fantasy and imagination in a wonderful way. Today's children will be drawn into the reality of events described in the scriptures. Ever true to the scriptural accounts, the authors have crafted delightful stories that will surely awaken children's vivid imaginations while teaching truths that will often sound familiar."

—TRUMAN AND ANN MADSEN
Truman Madsen is the bestselling author of *Joseph Smith, the Prophet*

"My dad and I read *At the Miracles of Jesus* together. First I'd read a chapter, and then he would. Now we're reading the next book. He says he feels the Spirit when we read. So do I."

—CASEY J., age 9

"My mom likes me to read before bed. I used to hate it, but the *Believe* books make reading fun and exciting. And they make you feel good inside, too."

—KADEN T., age 10

"Reading the *Believe* series with my tweens and my teens has been a big spiritual boost in our home—even for me! It always leaves me peaceful and more certain about what I believe."

—GLADYS A., age 43

"I love how Katie, Matthew, and Peter are connected to each other and to their grandma. These stories link children to their families, their ancestors, and on to the Savior. I heartily recommend them for any child, parent, or grandparent."

—ANNE S., age 50
Mother of ten, grandmother of nine (and counting)

When Esther
Saved Her People

Books in the *Believe and You're There* series

When Esther
Saved Her People

Book 8

ALICE W. JOHNSON & ALLISON H. WARNER

DESERET
BOOK

Salt Lake City, Utah

Library of Congress Cataloging-in-Publication Data

Johnson, Alice W.
  Believe and you're there when Esther saved her people / Alice W.
Johnson & Allison H. Warner ; illustrated by Casey Nelson.
    p. cm.
  Summary: Traveling into Grandma's newest painting, Katie, Matthew, and
Peter find themselves in the court of Queen Esther as she puts her life on the
line to try and save her people.
  ISBN 978-1-60641-815-4 (paperbound)
  1. Esther, Queen of Persia—Juvenile literature. 2. Bible stories, English.
I. Warner, Allison H. II. Nelson, Casey (Casey Shane), 1973– , ill.
III. Title.
  BS580.E8J64 2010
  222'.909505—dc22   2010019740

Printed in the United States of America
LSC Communications, Harrisonburg, VA   06/2016
10 9 8 7

Believe in the wonder,
Believe if you dare,
Believe in your heart,
Just believe . . . and you're there!

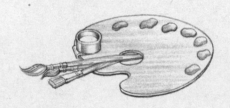

Contents

Chapter One

Katie's Situation

How does Grandma always know just the right time to unveil one of her magical paintings? That was the question running through the mind of twelve-year-old Katie as her mother pulled up to Grandma's house.

"Thanks, Mom," she chirped, leaping out of the car. Her two younger brothers, Matthew and Peter, bounded boisterously ahead, barely able to contain their excitement.

"Hey," their mother called after them, "don't I get a good-bye?"

"Good-bye, Mom," the boys hollered back from Grandma's front walk, offering an obligatory wave and blowing a kiss off the ends of their fingers.

But sensitive Katie ran around the car and

hugged her mother warmly. "See you tonight," she said, giving her mom a quick peck on the cheek before running to catch up with her brothers.

"Wait! Don't knock yet!" Katie implored her brothers, who danced anxiously on the front porch. "I want to get your opinion about something before we go in."

"Is it about your club again?" Peter asked impatiently.

"And what if it is?" Katie answered.

"Sis, we've had this conversation a million times," Matthew said wearily.

"*Twice* is more like it," Katie retorted. "But I still don't know what to do." She sounded discouraged.

The front door suddenly flew open and there stood Grandma, an enormous grin spread across her face. "What are you waiting for? Come on in," she beckoned.

"Well, we were ready to come in ages ago, but . . . ," Peter began, rolling his eyes. "Katie has this *huge* problem, which, in my opinion, isn't really a problem at all."

"That's because you aren't in the middle of it,"

Katie declared, pursing her lips and shooting her brother a look.

"Okay, guys, let's call a truce for now," Matthew begged, looking to Grandma for help.

Grandma took the hint. "Well this . . . uh . . . situation . . . ," she began, being very careful not to call it a problem. "This *situation* has obviously caused Katie some concern. Is that right?" She asked quickly before Peter could insert another comment.

Katie nodded, her eyes downcast.

"Well, why don't you come in, and we'll discuss things over some warm cinnamon rolls and milk. What do you say?"

"Why have we been standing out here all this time?" Peter blurted out. "Let's go!" He squeezed past Grandma and headed for the kitchen where the aroma of fresh-baked cinnamon rolls hung tantalizingly in the air.

"Hey, buddy," Matthew called out. "Don't touch those cinnamon rolls until we're all there." And he hustled behind Peter to stand guard.

Grandma put her arm around Katie and led her down the hall toward the kitchen. "Come on,

Katie, I'm sure we can help you find an answer to your pro—uh . . . your situation, that is."

Matthew and Peter already had four glasses filled with ice-cold milk sitting on the counter with a napkin next to each one. Peter ceremoniously presented Grandma with a spatula. "Okay, Grandma, we're all ready," he said, his mouth watering in anticipation.

As soon as the cinnamon rolls were served, Grandma turned to Katie and said, "All right. Let's all tackle this situation together and see if we can come up with a solution."

"Well," Katie began, "I belong to this club at school that meets every week. My friend Jenny has to bring her brother Charlie with her once a month while her mother is at work."

"That doesn't sound too bad," Grandma said.

"That part isn't so bad," Katie agreed. "The thing is, Charlie has Down syndrome. Sometimes he's a little noisy, and he likes to move around a lot and sit by different girls and take hold of their hands. Some of the girls don't want Charlie to come anymore. They're even talking about kicking Jenny out of the club."

"Oh, I see," Grandma spoke slowly. "You do have a problem."

"I told you! She has a *huge* problem!" Peter interjected.

"And *I* said most problems have a solution," Matthew said.

"Very wise, Matthew. He's right you know, kids. Most problems do have a solution. And, most of the time, we know in our hearts what's right to do."

"Oh, she knows what's right to do, all right,"

Peter said in an accusing tone. "She just doesn't want to do it."

"Peter!" Matthew scolded his brother.

"It's okay, Matthew," Katie said. "I hate to say it, but Peter's right." She flashed Peter a quick smile. "I don't care if Jenny brings Charlie. He has a funny sense of humor, and he is very sweet and friendly. But before I knew about it, a couple of club members convinced the president to ask Jenny not to come anymore. The club president is planning to talk to Jenny after our next meeting."

"Hmm, I see," Grandma mused thoughtfully. "So you have to work out a solution this weekend."

"Yes, I do," Katie replied. "And I think I have one."

"What is it?" Grandma asked.

"I've thought a lot about it, and I think I need to go to the club president and tell her I don't think it is right to exclude Jenny just because her brother is different."

"That sounds like a good plan to me," Matthew said encouragingly.

"I know it's the right thing to do, but I am so afraid to talk to the president."

"Why is that, dear?" Grandma asked.

"*Everyone* wants to be in this club. You have to be specially invited to join. And I don't want to get kicked out, too, for disagreeing with the president. I was so flattered just to be invited. And now . . ." Katie sounded genuinely sad at the thought of being excluded.

"I can see why you're afraid," Grandma said, offering her support. "I'll tell you what; why don't we go out to the art cottage? I think I was inspired to paint this new painting just for you, Katie."

At the mention of the art cottage, Peter and Matthew raced out the backdoor and down the flagstone path that led through Grandma's backyard.

Grandma held the door open for Katie and, linking arms, the two of them leisurely sauntered toward the art cottage. The back screen door slapped behind them as they left the house. Grandma chuckled as she watched her grandsons run, and, giving Katie a wink, Grandma declared, "And I think those two boys might just learn some important lessons, too!"

Chapter Two

The King's Word

On the large easel where Grandma's new paintings were always displayed, there was a large whiteboard with a hangman's game drawn on it. Peter's mouth dropped open as he stared at the whiteboard in disbelief. Katie sat down on the soft pillows laid out on the floor and tried to hide her disappointment. Pasting a weak smile on her face, she forced herself to say, "Oh, a game of hangman. This should be fun."

But Peter, in his usual forthright way, blurted out, "Hey, where's the new painting?"

Trying hard to keep a straight face, Grandma said, "I thought you might like to play a game of hangman this time."

"Instead of a painting?" Peter asked incredulously.

Grandma kept up her teasing just a little longer. "I thought you'd like a game of hangman before we start reading."

"Well . . . maybe . . . as long as it's fast," Peter replied with as much patience as he could muster.

Grandma smiled with a twinkle in her eye. "I think that's up to you, kids. Let's see how smart you are, shall we? This word is a name, and it has six letters. Matthew, you take the first guess."

Matthew sat up straight, studying the board. "I always start with a vowel, so I am going to guess 'A.'"

"No 'A,'" Grandma said and drew a circle for a head on the board. "Peter, do you have a guess?"

"Well, 'E' is another vowel, and there are two of them in my name, so I guess 'E,'" he declared confidently.

"Very good," Grandma smiled. "There are two 'Es' in this name, just like yours."

"Since it worked for Peter to guess a letter from his name, I'll try it too," Katie ventured. I guess 'T' because there is one in my name."

"Amazing!" Grandma said. "There is a 'T' right here. Matthew, I think it's your turn again."

"Okay," Matthew shrugged. "I'll try 'H' since my name has one."

"You've done it again!" Grandma cried in delight. "Okay," she took a step back and studied the board. "So far, our word looks like this. . . ."

E_THE_

"Any guesses?" Grandma looked at them expectantly.

A smile crept across Katie's face. "I know who it is. It's Esther."

"Yes, it is Queen Esther." Grandma removed the whiteboard to reveal a beautiful painting of Esther preparing to enter the king's court.

When they saw the painting on the easel, the three hopeful children gasped in relief.

"Okay, I'm ready! Let's get going!" Peter declared eagerly, sitting straight up on his pillow, his eyes dancing with anticipation.

"Go? But you just got here!" Grandma replied in surprise.

"That's not what he means, Grandma," Matthew jumped in. "He's just anxious to hear the story."

"You know me, Grandma, always on the move!" Peter reminded her.

Grandma chuckled as she reached for her glasses and settled down in her rocking chair. "Well then, here we go. If I had known my paintings would make you so eager to read the scriptures, I would have shared them with you long ago." She picked up her Bible from the table beside her and opened it to the first chapter of Esther in the Old Testament.

"Here we are. 'Now it came to pass . . . ,'" she began, "'When the king Ahasuerus sat on the throne of his kingdom, which was in Shushan the palace, in the third year of his reign, he made a feast unto all his princes and his servants.'"

As Grandma read, her grandchildren concentrated on the painting that was perched on the easel. Each time Grandma read to them from the scriptures, her painting of the story had come to life right before their eyes. And even though they had never been disappointed, the question always lingered: Will it happen again this time?

That question was quickly answered, and the children were again delighted. Matthew was the first to see the movement of the tiny figures in the painting. He nudged Katie and pointed to the servants gently swaying large feather fans above the king's head.

Matthew clasped Katie's hand in his and then looked to Peter, who winked and locked his hand with his brother's.

A shiver of excitement ran through Katie as she

reached up and pressed her finger into the corner of the canvas. As her hand disappeared into the painting a sudden burst of air surrounded the children and, with a loud whooshing noise, it lifted them up and out of the art cottage. Rushing wind swirled swiftly around the three children and, in no time at all, they gently descended in front of the gates of the Shushan Palace.

"That's more exciting than any carnival ride I've ever been on," Peter said with a wide grin on his face.

"No kidding!" Matthew enthusiastically agreed. Then, "Wh-o-o-oa!" he said, pointing at the immense palace that loomed above them. "Would you look at that!"

"Wow!" Peter echoed, straining to see the top of the palace, which stood atop a rocky hill that rose from the valley floor.

"It looks like a bunch of Greek temples all hooked together. It's huge!" Katie said.

"It looks like its own little city," Matthew mused.

"Why are all those people crowded over there

by the palace gates?" Peter wondered. "I'm going to go check it out." And off he ran to investigate.

"We'd better hurry if we're going to catch up with him," Katie said, smiling at her brother's unbridled curiosity.

When they reached him, Peter was already chatting animatedly with a young Persian girl in the crowd.

"Hi," he waved to them cheerily. "This is Ashtel," and he gestured to the girl beside him. "Ashtel, this is my brother, Matthew, and my sister, Katie."

"Hello. It is nice to meet you. You surely have a friendly brother," Ashtel said to Matthew and Katie, smiling shyly.

"It's nice to meet you too," Matthew said, smiling back. "What's going on?" he asked, pointing to all the people gathered at the gate.

"The king has posted another decree," Ashtel began.

"I can't see what is says," Peter declared.

"I cannot, either," she said. "It is too crowded. We will have to wait until some of the people leave.

But I know what the last decree said. It declared that Queen Vashti was banished."

"Banished?" Peter sounded confused. "What does that mean?"

"It means that she was sent away from this kingdom and that she must never return." Ashtel spoke sadly as she explained the terrible, lifelong punishment.

"Why on earth would she be banished by the king?" Katie asked incredulously.

"Well, the king was hosting a royal feast for the princes and nobles from the surrounding provinces," Ashtel began. "He summoned Queen Vashti to come before his guests and display her beauty. But she refused the king's request."

"Why would he banish her just for that?" Matthew wanted to know. "Maybe she wasn't feeling well, or maybe she was just having a bad hair day or something."

"Maybe, but her refusal embarrassed him in front of his important guests, and it made him very angry," Ashtel explained.

"Angry enough to get *rid* of her?" Peter asked.

"The king and his advisors thought that Queen

Vashti set a bad example for all the women in the kingdom," Ashtel responded.

"Hmmm. I guess when the king asks you to do something, you better do it, no matter what!" Peter said. "Even if you *are* the queen!"

"*Especially* if you are the queen," Ashtel said. "You see, here in Shushan, the king's word is the law. And everyone—no matter who you are—must obey."

Chapter Three

A Servant to the Queen

"Do you live here in Shushan?" Katie asked Ashtel.

"Actually, I live right here in the palace," Ashtel replied.

"Are you a princess?" Peter asked, wide-eyed.

"Oh, no," she assured her new friends quickly. "I am a servant. I have just returned from the market where I purchased fragrant oils for the women of the palace."

"I have never been in a palace before. Where I come from, we don't even *have* palaces," Peter told Ashtel.

"Do you come from far away?" she asked him.

Before he could answer, Katie broke in, "Yes, we come from very far away. And we are only here visiting for a short while," she smiled sweetly, hoping Ashtel wouldn't ask her exactly where they lived.

Matthew took it from there. "So you can see why we are so amazed at the size of this palace. It almost looks like a little city."

"Yes, it is just that," Ashtel agreed. "My family and I all live inside the walls of the palace. Each one of us has a special job to do. Come," she invited the three siblings. "I will give you a tour. Do just as I say, and no one will even know you are visiting. But," she said skeptically as she looked at Katie's blonde hair, "perhaps you should wear this head scarf." And she quickly removed an extra scarf that had been over her shoulder.

She deftly draped the scarf over Katie's head and flung one end of it over Katie's left shoulder. "There!" she said with satisfaction. "Now everyone will assume you are all servants, just like me."

Ashtel led the children along the winding path that rimmed the outside of the massive palace walls. The three children followed, awestruck by the grandeur of the palace. "These buildings look just like the ones in our ancient history book at school," Matthew breathed to Katie. "I can't believe I'm really seeing this in person!"

Soon, they reached a heavy wooden gate in the wall. Ashtel knocked three times, and the gate swung inward. A guard admitted them, nodding to Ashtel in recognition. They entered a small courtyard with narrow paths leading away from it in all directions.

"How do you know where to go? This looks like a maze," Matthew said as his eyes passed from path to path.

"I used to get lost, but now I am accustomed to it," Ashtel answered. "Follow me."

They headed down one of the stone pathways. Very shortly, it opened into a magnificent garden. The children gasped at the splendor laid out before them. In stark contrast to the dry, rugged landscape beyond the palace walls, lush green shrubs, tall cypress trees, and gurgling waterways created a luxurious, calming retreat.

"Ashtel!" someone hollered.

They turned to see a boy waving and running toward them. Ashtel smiled and eagerly returned his wave. "This is my brother, Hiram," she explained. "Hiram, this is Katie, Matthew, and Peter. They are visiting here in Shushan and have never seen a palace before."

"This is some amazing place!" Peter said enthusiastically.

"Yes, it is," Hiram agreed. "Even if you live here, you never really get used to it."

"We would love to show it to you, but first we must attend to our responsibilities," Ashtel said dutifully.

"I'm a great worker," Peter assured them. "Matthew and I could help, if you like."

"Perhaps that would be best. There are many servants in the king's court. You would fit right in," Hiram said, warming to the idea.

"Katie could come with me, and the boys could go with you, Hiram," Ashtel suggested.

"Oh, that reminds me! Hegai is looking for you. He is waiting for you to return with the oils," Hiram informed Ashtel.

"Oh, yes! I am afraid I lost track of the time," Ashtel said anxiously. "Come, Katie, let us hurry. We will see you when we have finished our duties, boys." And she and Katie rushed away.

Katie followed closely behind Ashtel through the mazelike corridors of the palace. The walls of the corridors were made of large stone slabs, each carved with an intricate scene. All depicted servants waiting on the king. Some showed attendants bringing towels and ointments to him. Others showed them lavishing him with food and wine. Katie was concentrating so hard on the scenes, she almost ran into Ashtel who had stopped at the entrance to the women's quarters.

"You remember I told you that Queen Vashti was banished?" Ashtel whispered to Katie in a low voice. Katie nodded silently. "After that happened, the king sent out a decree for all the beautiful young maidens in the surrounding provinces to be gathered to the palace. The king then selected one of them to be his new queen."

"Did many come?" Katie asked.

"Oh, yes." Ashtel led Katie to a secluded private garden near the entrance to the women's quarters. They sat together on a stone bench at the edge of a small pond as Ashtel continued her story.

"Many came and lived in the king's house. They

were all beautiful, but not many were as beautiful on the inside as they were on the outside."

"I've known people like that. They are not very pleasant to be around," Katie responded.

"That is true," Ashtel agreed. "Which is why the king loved a maiden named Esther above all the others. She is not only beautiful, she is very kind, and she obtained grace and favor in his sight. So he placed the royal crown upon her head and made her his queen."

"You are an attendant to the queen?" Katie asked, filled with admiration for Ashtel.

"Yes, I am. Hegai, the keeper of the women, appointed seven of us to be Esther's maids when she was made queen. I have served her ever since," Ashtel said. "I consider it a great honor to serve Queen Esther."

"I feel that I have kept you from your duties. You have been so kind to me. Please, let me help you finish your work for the day," Katie offered.

"Thank you," Ashtel answered gratefully. "I would like that, Katie. And I can show you the queen's quarters as we work."

"Doesn't she live with the king?" Katie asked, sounding confused.

"Oh, no. Here in the palace, the women live separately from the men. The only way the queen can see the king is if she is summoned to his presence. If she goes to him without being summoned, he can have her put to death."

"Death? Would he really do that?" Katie asked, horrified at the thought.

"He has the power to choose. If she goes into him and he holds out his sceptre to her, her life is spared. But if not, she could be put to death," Ashtel explained solemnly.

My, things sure are different here in Persia, Katie thought to herself. *Ashtel wasn't kidding when she said everyone must do exactly what the king wants. I had better watch myself.*

"Come," Ashtel beckoned Katie, "we will work together. When we have finished we will find out what the boys have been doing all afternoon."

Chapter Four

Haman's Evil Plot

Katie and Ashtel delivered the perfumed oils to Hegai and then began washing the smooth stone floors in the queen's bedchamber. As the girls were working, Hiram led Matthew and Peter through a maze of walkways and corridors on their way to the grand throne room. There they were to wash and oil the stone walls to bring out their rich color.

"Boy, everything here has to do with the king, doesn't it?" Peter observed, as they made their way through more corridors decorated with carvings of servants waiting on the king.

"Yes, that is true," Hiram concurred. "King Ahasuerus has supreme authority over everyone in the kingdom."

"Did he really fight this wild beast?" Matthew

asked, standing in front of a large, colorful mosaic depicting the king in fierce battle with a winged creature.

"I don't think so," Hiram replied, shaking his head. "I think that carving just represents the king's power and dominion over everything, even wild animals. His word is law and his power is absolute," Hiram answered.

"Well, he sure has a terrific house—or palace, I guess I should say," Peter remarked.

"And there is much more to this palace that you have not yet seen. Come, let me show you King's Gate. Then, we will go to Throne Hall and you can help me with my duties there," Hiram said.

As they approached King's Gate, the moaning sounds of a man filled the air.

"Why is that man crying like that? Is he in pain?" Matthew asked Hiram.

"Someone must be in mourning," Hiram answered.

"Mourning for what?"

"I don't know," Hiram shrugged.

As they rounded the corner, the wailing man came into view.

"What is he wearing?" Peter asked, staring at the wailing man, who was dressed in loose, tattered robes and whose head was covered with ashes.

Hiram didn't answer. Instead, he ran directly to the moaning man. "Mordecai!" Hiram exclaimed, taking the man by the shoulders. "What is it? Why are you mourning? What has happened?"

"Can I take you into my confidence?" The man called Mordecai lifted his head and spoke to Hiram in earnest.

"Yes, of course," Hiram assured him.

Mordecai looked past Hiram to Matthew and Peter. He looked them up and down with a measure of distrust in his eyes. "And what about them?" He questioned Hiram. "Can they be trusted?"

"I am very trustworthy! Cross my heart!" Peter said, smiling at Mordecai warmly.

Hiram and Mordecai looked at each other, completely confused by Peter's statement.

Matthew jumped in to explain. "That's just Peter's way of saying that he gives you his word. You are safe with us."

"I will vouch for them. I believe them to be very trustworthy," Hiram promised Mordecai.

"Well," Mordecai began, "Haman has just posted a new decree. It orders that all the Jews in the kingdom be killed."

"What? So that must be why so many people were crowded at the gate," Hiram said, as the news settled on him. "But *we* are Jews!"

"Yes. I am, you are, and so are many other faithful servants to the king," Mordecai said to Hiram quietly. "And we all are condemned to die."

"Even you?" Hiram was astonished. "But you

have been so loyal to the king! Surely the king re-
members that it was you who discovered the plot
of the court chamberlains, when they sought to
take the king's life. Had you not told Esther about
the plot, the king surely would have been killed.
He was very grateful to you. He even had it written
in the book of the chronicles so that your loyalty
and bravery would never be forgotten. I do not

29

understand why he would ever sign such a decree!" Hiram declared with feeling.

"It is not the king's idea," Mordecai quickly explained. "Haman is responsible for this. All the other advisors in the king's court bow down whenever Haman passes by. But I cannot. Like all faithful Jews, I will bow down only to my God." Mordecai spoke sincerely, and then, as if overcome by hopelessness, he resumed his loud lamenting.

"Who is this Haman?" Peter whispered to Hiram. "He must be a really mean guy."

"Haman is the king's chief advisor. The king made Haman ruler over all the princes in the land. Basically, Haman can do whatever he pleases in this kingdom. He is a very proud and powerful man," Hiram explained.

Mordecai's wailing subsided. "I knew there would be a problem when I heard Haman ask his servants who I was and why I did not bow down to him when he passed by. But I didn't know it would come to this."

"Matthew!" At the sound of his name, Matthew reeled around to see who could possibly be calling him. It was Katie! She was hurrying toward him.

Ashtel followed close behind, a troubled look on her face.

Matthew sensed the girls' anxiety. "Are you two all right?"

"Oh, Matthew," Katie began. "Queen Esther can hear Mordecai wailing all the way from her quarters. Mordecai is her uncle, and she loves him dearly. She is extremely worried about him."

Ashtel picked up the tale. "She has sent Hatach to see what the trouble is, but we couldn't wait to learn what has happened, so we came quickly to see for ourselves."

Hiram began to recount the terrible news, "Haman has persuaded the king to sign a decree ordering all the Jews in Shushan be put to death."

"To death! But why?" Ashtel could hardly believe what she was hearing.

Hiram recounted the whole story, just as he had heard it from Mordecai. Ashtel and Katie listened intently, their eyes growing wider at every detail of the disturbing news.

"Surely, there is something we can do," Ashtel cried, on the verge of tears. "Why would the king agree to this awful scheme?"

31

"Many loyal Jews live in Persia," Hiram informed Katie, Matthew, and Peter. "We honor and obey the laws of the land, but we also live by our Jewish laws and customs. Although we are different from Persians in some ways, we are alike in many, many more. The king does not understand Jews, because he does not know who we are. I'll bet he doesn't even know that loyal Mordecai and beautiful Queen Esther are Jewish, too!" Now Hiram was almost wailing like Mordecai.

Peter, whose face was turning red with anger and frustration, blurted out, "Something should be done to Haman, that mean old man!"

"Yes, something must be done," Ashtel agreed. "Mordecai, Hatach will be here any moment. You send word with him to the queen, and we will see what happens. Come, Katie, we should hurry back to the queen's chambers."

They hurried away, leaving Matthew, Peter, and Hiram watching Mordecai as he slowly paced up and down the street, a strategy forming clearly in his mind.

Chapter Five

For Such a Time as This

In the courtyard that opened onto King's Gate, Ashtel and Katie crossed paths with Hatach, who hurried past them, intent on his errand.

"That was lucky," Ashtel whispered, as they watched him disappear through the gates. "He didn't notice us at all. Let us hurry back before we are missed."

At the servants' entrance to the queen's quarters, Ashtel lifted the latch of the ornate wooden door, and she and Katie slipped inside without being seen.

"It is time for me to set the pillows on the couches in the queen's chamber. In the afternoon, she and her friends will want a place to rest," Ashtel told Katie.

Ashtel led Katie into a courtyard that featured a small pool of clear blue water. Ringing the pool were several benches and lounging couches. A large, round opening overhead revealed a brilliant sky with white, fluffy clouds gently floating in it.

Ashtel went purposefully to a large chest in the corner of the courtyard, tucked behind a carved wooden screen. It was filled with intricately embroidered pillows and soft linen blankets. Ashtel gave Katie a stack of pillows to carry, and she picked up three cream-colored blankets.

"We'll put a blanket and pillow on each couch. Then we'll set golden goblets on the tables near each couch. Soon the servants from the palace kitchen will bring trays of food filled with pomegranates, pistachios, dates, raisins, and almonds," Ashtel explained to Katie.

"What shall I do when the royal women come in?" Katie asked, tucking her stray blonde hairs beneath her head scarf and trying not to sound as nervous as she felt.

"Here," Ashtel said as she handed her a large feather fan. "Stand at the head of this couch, and gently wave the fan over the head of Queen Esther.

But try not to drop it on her," Ashtel teasingly warned.

"I'll do my best to hang on," Katie assured her, smiling at the very thought.

At that moment, the door opened. Queen Esther entered, accompanied by a half-dozen attendants. Esther was the most beautiful woman Katie had ever seen. Some of her dark brown hair was arranged on top of her head, and the rest billowed in loose curls around her neck. Her long, flowing, purple silk dress draped softly to the floor, and it was cinched at the waist with a wide belt, studded with precious gems and colorful beads. Esther moved gracefully across the room toward the couch, where Katie stood ready with her fan. The young queen smiled at Katie as she sat down and reclined on the couch.

"Ashtel," her kind voice summoned Katie's new friend. "Come, play a melody on your flute for me. My heart is heavy with concern for my uncle, Mordecai. A soothing melody will help calm my fears."

"Yes, Queen Esther," Ashtel responded, remembering that Esther awaited news about why her uncle was in mourning. Ashtel retrieved what appeared to be a wooden recorder from behind the carved screen and settled on a small bench near the queen. She began playing a sweet, haunting song that seemed to fill the courtyard with serenity.

Katie slowly waved the fan over Esther's head, knowing the heaviness that must be in the queen's heart. Esther seemed to relax as the music floated all around her.

A loud knock broke the spell. Esther sat up quickly, looking expectantly toward the door. The door opened, and Hatach entered the room.

"Your Majesty," he said, greeting the queen with a deep bow.

"What news do you have for me, Hatach?" Esther asked, her voice filled with worry.

"Mordecai sits in sackcloth and ashes outside King's Gate because Haman has convinced the king to put to death all the Jews in Persia. Furthermore, Haman has pledged to pay the king's treasuries ten thousand talents of silver for the lives of the Jews."

"But we have done nothing to him! Why would

Haman do such a thing?" Esther asked, deeply troubled by this news.

"Haman is furious," Hatach explained, "because Mordecai will not bow down to worship him. As you know, Mordecai bows only before his God, the Great Jehovah," Hatach went on. "Here is a copy of the decree that has been sent to all the provinces in the land."

Esther read the decree in utter disbelief. "What does Mordecai think we can do to reverse this decree?"

Hatach spoke almost apologetically. "Well, he wants you, the queen, to reveal to the king that you are Jewish, and petition him in behalf of your people."

Esther looked stunned by Mordecai's request. "Hatach," she said with genuine dismay in her voice, "go and tell Mordecai that I have not been called to come unto the king for thirty days. The law declares that anyone who goes into the king's inner court without being summoned by the king will be put to death. We all know that.

"If the king holds out his sceptre to the person who has come uninvited, only then will that

person's life be spared." Esther sounded frightened at the prospect of risking her life. "So please tell Mordecai I simply cannot do as he has asked. I am sure he will understand."

"I see," said Hatach. "I will go and tell Mordecai your response. Then I shall return." And he quietly left the courtyard.

Esther sat silently, a veil of sadness passing over her face. "Ashtel, please continue playing that beautiful melody."

As Ashtel resumed playing her flute, Esther arose from her couch and walked slowly around the pool, carrying the dreadful decree that ordered all Jews to be put to death.

Katie stood quietly watching Esther. She could almost feel the weight of Esther's heavy burden. The fate of Esther's people lay in her hands, yet she also faced the possibility of her own death if she intervened! What should she do?

A loud knock on the door interrupted Ashtel's melody. Hatach, out of breath, entered and bowed again before the queen.

"Your Majesty," he greeted her.

"What did my uncle say?" Esther inquired hesitantly, as if she were afraid to hear his response.

Hatach took a deep breath and answered slowly, so that Mordecai's message could not be mistaken. "Mordecai sends this important reply to the queen. He says that you are not to think that because you are in the king's palace, that you shall escape the same fate as all the Jews. Mordecai says that if you say nothing, God will find another way to save our people, but surely you, and your father's house, shall be destroyed."

Hatach paused for a moment, and looked deep into Esther's eyes, "And then, Your Majesty, Mordecai wanted me to ask you this vital question: Who knows whether you are come to the kingdom for such a time as this?"

"Thank you," Esther whispered. "You may go."

The room was silent. Esther was struck to the core by the words of her uncle. For now she was faced with a very difficult choice. She had been asked to be an instrument in God's hands to help save His chosen people, risking her own life in the process.

According to Mordecai, if she refused, God

would surely find another way to save the Jews. But what if she, Esther, was come for this very moment? What if she missed this important opportunity to serve God? What if Esther refused to do the hard things that were part of her mission on earth? As Mordecai said, God would find another way to save the Jews. But what would become of Esther?

"Queen Esther?" Ashtel said softly.

"Yes," Esther replied.

"I know a song that may ease your troubled mind. May I sing it for you?"

"Yes, Ashtel. I would love to hear such a song."

As Katie gently fanned the uneasy queen, Ashtel sang a song to comfort kind Esther.

> *We are sent here with a purpose*
> *A mission to fulfill,*
> *A plan to serve Jehovah,*
> *To carry out His will.*
> *And someday we'll stand before Him,*
> *Our lives complete at last.*
> *Our words and deeds will answer all*
> *The questions He will ask:*
> *Were you true unto Jehovah?*
> *Did you worship Him in faith?*

Did you do all that He asked of you,
And serve Him all your days?
Was your heart filled with the courage
To do Jehovah's will?
For though our trials may be great,
Yet we must serve Him still.

Chapter Six

"If I Perish, I Perish"

Ashtel finished her song. The closing words, "For though our trials may be great, yet we must serve Him still," seemed to hang heavy in the air. Esther bowed her head and sat still in the hushed courtyard. All that could be heard was the gentle lapping of water in the courtyard pool. But still the turmoil in Esther's heart remained.

Katie and Ashtel watched from behind the royal couch, not daring to move a muscle. After several minutes, Esther resolutely squared her shoulders and raised her head. A new, serene strength radiated unmistakably from her countenance.

"Please summon Hatach," Esther instructed Ashtel with resolve.

"Yes, Your Majesty," Ashtel answered, and

quickly called to Hatach, who was pacing in the outer corridor.

Esther stood at the side of her couch, awaiting Hatach. He bowed when he reached the queen, prepared to carry out her wishes.

"I now know what I must do," she began. "Go, gather together all the Jews that are present in Shushan, and fast ye for me, and neither eat nor drink three days, night or day: I also and my maidens will fast likewise; and so will I go in unto the king."

"But, Your Majesty, you know the law!" Hatach protested.

Esther raised her hand to quiet Hatach's objections. And courageously, the queen declared, "If I perish, I perish."

"Yes, Your Majesty," Hatach said, inspired by Esther's brave reply. "I will inform Mordecai of your intentions." He left the courtyard and hurried to deliver the news to Mordecai.

"Come, we will prepare for our fast. Ashtel, would you please come into my bedchamber shortly, with your flute? Your lovely music is such a comfort to me." With that, Esther and her handmaids left the courtyard, retiring to the queen's private chamber.

"Katie, I must soon go to the queen," Ashtel said.

Katie thought quickly about the circumstances and declared, "My brothers and I will leave Shushan until your fast is over. But we will return in three days. Would that be all right?"

"I would like that. We have just begun to become good friends, Katie. Please return. I will meet you at King's Gate in three days," Ashtel assured her. "Come, let us find Hiram and your brothers."

When the boys were not to be found inside the palace, the girls headed toward King's Gate. News of the fast was spreading to the Jews gathered at the gate. A ray of hope was beginning to shine through the gloom that had surrounded them since the awful decree had been made.

Catching a glimpse of Peter's curly hair, Katie was filled with relief. "Matthew! Peter!" she called to her brothers excitedly.

"Hi, Sis! We've been having a great time with Hiram. He has shown us some of the most amazing things!" Matthew's reply was enthusiastic.

"For instance," Peter could hardly contain himself, "did you know that the king has a whole army with the coolest bows and arrows ever?" Peter was always very interested in weapons.

"It is *so* good to see you guys," Katie spoke to her brothers as if they'd been apart for much more than just an afternoon. "I suppose you've heard about the three-day fast?"

"Yes, we have. The Jews are spreading the news as quickly as they can," Hiram answered. "Queen Esther sure is brave!"

"Oh, Esther! I must get back to the queen!" Ashtel said, reminded by Hiram of the waiting queen. "Katie, my friend, come back in three days and we will finish our palace tour."

Ashtel and Hiram waved good-bye and disappeared into the palace.

"That was a close one!" Peter breathed. "No food or water for three days? We'd all be dead!"

"We need to plan our strategy," Matthew said, weighing all their possible options carefully in his mind. "I think it might be good to go back to Grandma's and come back when this has all blown over."

"Exactly what I've been thinking, Matthew," Katie concurred. "Great minds think alike!"

"So do hungry stomachs," Peter added. "I think we should head back before all this fasting starts. Besides, maybe Grandma will have some lunch ready for us!"

"I'm with you, bro," Katie said, offering her hands to her brothers. As soon the children linked hands, the palace of Shushan disappeared and the smell of paint in Grandma's art cottage filled the air swirling around them. They felt the soft pillows cushion their bodies as they landed softly on the floor at Grandma's feet.

"'So Mordecai went his way, and did according to all that Esther had commanded him.'" Grandma rocked gently back and forth as she finished the chapter.

"Grandma, I am so, so, sorry to interrupt, but all that talk about fasting has made me very hungry," Peter said, in almost a moan. "Do you think we could have a little snack before you finish?"

"Why is it I don't think that much about food until someone says I can't have any?" Matthew wondered out loud.

Grandma smiled. "I don't know, Matthew, but that's sure true for me too! I think we could rustle up a little snack. Let's all go see what I have in my kitchen."

"I saw some Oreos in your cupboard. I'll go get them, okay?" Peter called over his shoulder as he bounded for the back door.

Grandma, Katie, and Matthew heard the back screen door slap before they were even halfway across the yard. When they reached the kitchen, Peter had already laid the package of cookies on the table and poured four glasses of milk, with only one small spill.

"I can't imagine why anyone would want to go without food or drink for three whole days. That is just plain crazy!" Peter blurted out, while dipping a cookie in milk and popping it whole into his mouth. A satisfied smile crept across his face.

"Grandma, why did the Jews fast anyway?" Matthew's question was earnest and sincere. He twisted the top off his Oreo and ate the crunchy side first, saving the filling side for last.

"That's a very good question, Matthew," Grandma began. "All through the Old Testament, prophets taught about fasting and prayer as a way to gain spiritual strength."

"Strength?" Peter exclaimed. "I thought skipping food just made you weak."

"Well, it does make you aware of how frail and weak the body is," Grandma agreed.

"But when you don't have to think about eating, it frees your mind to think about other more important things, right?" Matthew added.

"That's right," Grandma confirmed. "I like to fill my mind with prayers when I'm fasting. Otherwise, if I fast without praying, all I think about is being hungry. Then, like Peter said, you're just skipping food. But if I pray *and* fast, I rely on God for my strength. And He makes me feel much stronger than food does!"

"Hey, mind over matter! Or mind over *body*, I guess I should say," Peter said, a light turning on in his mind.

"That's right, Peter! When you fast and pray, answers to your questions become clearer in your mind, and Heavenly Father blesses you with His Spirit," Grandma said.

"No wonder Esther wanted the Jews to fast for three days. She was facing a serious problem, and she needed the faith of all the Jews to strengthen her. Now I understand why she made such a request," Katie said with understanding, as she set her cookie down. "I think I'll wait to eat until we find out what happens to Esther. After all, Ashtel has to fast for three days. I only have to fast for three hours."

"Ashtel? That is an unusual name. Is she a friend from school?" Grandma asked.

"Well, not exactly," Katie stammered, forcing an innocent smile. "She's just a friend I met."

Chapter Seven

Praying for a Miracle

"I'd say it's time to get back to our adventure," Peter told Grandma, as he wiped up his crumbs and headed for the back door.

"All of life is an adventure to you," Grandma quipped. "Well, Matthew and Katie, what are you two waiting for? Where is your spirit of adventure? Let's go!" She waved them all out the door and followed her three grandchildren through the yard, toward the door of the art cottage.

Peter got there first. "Believe!" he called out from the front step of the cottage.

"In the wonder," Grandma, Katie, and Matthew returned.

"Believe!" he said again.

"If you dare," they called out in unison.

"Believe!" Peter shouted a third time.

"In your heart!" was the reply.

"Just believe," cried Peter.

And everyone finished together, "And you're there!"

Peter threw open the door and headed for his floor pillow. Katie and Matthew followed his lead, and Grandma resumed her spot in the overstuffed rocking chair.

"Okay, kids. When we left off, Esther had just sent word to Mordecai, instructing all the Jews to fast with her for three days. Let's see what happens now." Grandma adjusted her glasses and started reading.

"'Now it came to pass on the third day, that Esther put on her royal apparel . . . ,'" Grandma began.

Right on cue, the painting came to life. Tiny figures scurried around King's Gate. Katie glanced at Grandma, who read on, seemingly unaware of the activity on the canvas beside her. But her grandchildren watched every tiny movement with anticipation. When they were sure Grandma was thoroughly engrossed in the story, they quietly

52

locked hands and Peter plunged his hand into the canvas.

"Oh," Katie exclaimed breathlessly, as her feet touched the ground outside King's Gate. "That was quick."

"Katie! Matthew! Peter!" Ashtel and Hiram ran toward them.

"I knew you would return," Ashtel cried, as she embraced Katie warmly.

Peter put out his hand to her. "A handshake will do for me, thank you," he declared. "I don't like all that huggy stuff."

"Very well, a handshake then." Ashtel reached out her hand to Peter, and then offered it to Matthew. "Let us leave the 'huggy stuff' to the girls." She smiled affectionately at Peter.

"Where did you come from?" Hiram asked. "It seemed you appeared out of nowhere. We just turned our backs for a moment and there you were."

"Amazing, isn't it?" Matthew replied with a wide smile. "Now you see us, now you don't!" he joked.

Hiram laughed. "Come on, boys, wherever you

came from. We do not have time to stand around here. Let us go quickly. We must prepare the king's robes." Matthew and Peter waved good-bye to their sister and followed Hiram to the king's inner rooms.

"Come, Katie," Ashtel beckoned. "Esther is ending her fast today, and who knows what that will bring."

"Did you really go without food for three days?" Katie asked Ashtel.

Ashtel nodded.

"It must have been hard. How did you do it?" she asked Ashtel with admiration.

"It was hard, especially at first," Ashtel began. "But as time went on, I began thinking about my mother and father and Hiram, and all the other Jews in danger of dying. I thought how much I love Queen Esther, who has always been so kind to me. I don't want her to die, either!

"I knew if I joined my faith with the faith of Esther and all the Jews that perhaps the Lord would perform a miracle. So I prayed along with them, and that made me feel stronger. And the stronger I felt, the less hungry I was."

Ashtel and Katie walked quickly through the now familiar hallways to the queen's private rooms. Upon entering, they were met with a flurry of activity.

Hegai, the keeper of the women, summoned Ashtel. "Esther has completed her fast and has decided now to go unto the king. She will need your help to make the necessary preparations."

"I will attend her immediately," Ashtel said. "Come, Katie, let us hurry. The queen will be looking for me."

The girls entered Esther's luxurious suite of dressing rooms. One of her handmaids was putting the finishing touches on an elegant hairstyle. Esther's long, dark, silky hair fell in soft ringlets past the middle of her back. The front of her hair was pulled up and away from her face, making her expressive eyes stand out even more.

"That is beautiful," she approved, gazing at her reflection in the polished glass. "I am ready to dress now."

Esther's attendants fastened her royal robes over her white pleated underdress. The richly embroidered deep blue silk draped beautifully across her shoulders, cascading to the floor, and the fine ruby ornaments dangling from her neckline glistened and shimmered in the light. A gold crown was placed on Esther's head and pinned in place.

Though Esther's beauty was breathtaking, and her royal apparel exquisite, Katie knew that her real beauty shone from within. It was a beauty that revealed the inner strength of a woman filled with faith and the determination to serve God.

Ashtel motioned to Katie. "I will carry one side of her robes and you carry the other," she said softly.

Ashtel, Katie, and several handmaids followed behind as Esther led the way to the king's house. At the entrance, Esther paused, bowed her head, and stood in a silent prayer. After a moment she raised her head and spoke to her attendants. "Wait for me here. If it is God's will, I shall return."

Then she called Ashtel to her. "Pray for me and all our people. For only God can deliver us. Now, please lift my robes and accompany me."

Ashtel and Katie again raised the ends of Esther's royal robe, and followed her along the marble hallway within the king's quarters. The entrance to the king's inner court was marked by two large marble pillars from which hung flowing silken drapes.

Katie and Ashtel walked behind the queen between the marble pillars and into the inner court. A hush fell when Esther entered. The servants and king's advisors quickly parted, clearing a path so that Esther could be seen by the king where he sat on his throne in the royal throne room. The king's magnificent gold throne sat under a large canopy draped with heavy curtains.

Slowly, but with great courage, Esther stood in the courtyard so that she could be seen by the king. Although she knew the risk she was taking, she stood calmly and met his searching gaze.

A slight smile crossed the king's face, and Esther knew she had gained favor in his sight. He lowered the golden sceptre that was in his hand toward her. Esther returned his smile and then walked from the inner court into the throne room. She stepped up to the king and touched the point of the sceptre, signaling her gratitude.

"What is it you want, Queen Esther?" the king asked. "Whatever it is, it shall be given you, even to the half of my kingdom."

Esther answered with only one request. "If it seem good unto the king, let the king and Haman come this day unto the banquet that I have prepared for him."

"Send word to Haman to come quickly," the king ordered an attendant. "Queen Esther has prepared a banquet for us."

"Thank you. I shall await your arrival." Esther bowed to the king and left the throne room, the Spirit of God warming her heart and assuring her that she had done the right thing.

Chapter Eight

Restless and Unable to Sleep

In her royal dining chamber, Esther inspected every detail of the feast that was laid upon the dining cloth spread over the low table that spanned almost the length of the chamber. Along the table were large bronze platters of roasted meat, round crusty loaves of fresh-baked bread, gold bowls overflowing with fresh fruit, and casks of delicious drink.

"I hope all is to your liking," Ashtel said, as she set a golden goblet at each place on the table and arranged a lounging couch near each goblet.

"Yes, Ashtel. It all looks wonderful," Esther said. "Thank you."

Three loud knocks sounded on the heavy carved chamber doors. The doors swung open to reveal the king, arrayed in finely woven turquoise robes that were fastened in the front with a heavy gold chain. On his right hand, he wore a ring in the shape of a lion's head with two large rubies for the eyes. He strode confidently into the room and stopped as he came face to face with Esther. Esther bowed her head slightly to welcome him. "Thank you for coming, Your Majesty."

Haman entered the room and stood behind the king. He bowed low to Queen Esther.

"Welcome," she said. "Please sit down." Esther pointed to the lounging couches. She then motioned to her servants, who poured the beverages and began serving food from the platters to her guests. Ashtel and Katie stood quietly behind Esther, ready to do her bidding.

As the meal neared an end, the king took one last drink, set down his goblet, and turned to Esther. "What is your petition?" he asked. "What is your request? It shall be granted you, even to half the kingdom."

Esther answered, "If I have found favour in the sight of the king, and if it please the king to grant my petition, . . . let the king and Haman come to another banquet tomorrow that I shall prepare for them, and I will make my petition then, as the king has said."

The king gazed at Esther, remembering the first time he had seen her. Even now he was moved by her beauty and grace. How could he refuse her? He leaned toward her and said, smiling, "I will grant thy request."

"Thank you," she answered him warmly, gratitude filling her eyes.

"Until tomorrow, then," he said, rising from the table. "Come, Haman, we shall return tomorrow." The king strode from the room, Haman following close behind.

Meanwhile, Hiram, Matthew, and Peter were watching and waiting at King's Gate for news from Katie and Ashtel.

"Look!" Hiram said, pointing behind Matthew and Peter.

Matthew and Peter turned and saw Haman and his attendants striding importantly through the gate, their heads held high. As Haman passed through the crowd, all the people scurried out of his way and bowed low to him. All the people, that is, except for Mordecai. Mordecai sat firmly without moving, refusing to bow before Haman. When Haman saw that Mordecai still defied his order, his eyes blazed with anger and indignation. With great effort he restrained himself and returned to his home.

"Hiram," a servant of the king approached the boy with a letter in his hand.

"The king desires you to take this letter to Haman."

"I will go immediately," Hiram replied. "Come, Matthew and Peter, we will go together."

When they arrived at Haman's house, he was sitting surrounded by friends in the front courtyard with his wife, Zeresh. Haman's servants served drink and fruit to his guests as they talked.

"Wait," said Peter. "Let's see what he is saying." They stood out of sight, right near the courtyard entrance, and listened to Haman brag to his friends.

"Now that I have found favor with the king, I am a very rich man," he boasted. "The king has elevated me above all his other princes and servants. Today, Queen Esther let no man except me come in with the king to the banquet she had prepared for him. And tomorrow she has invited me to dine with her and the king again." Haman broke open a pomegranate and held it in his hands, and said bitterly, "But all this means nothing to me as long as I see Mordecai, the Jew, sitting at King's Gate, refusing to bow to me."

Matthew looked at Peter and Hiram fearfully. "I can't believe . . . ," he started to say, but Hiram stopped him, shaking his head and raising his fingers to his lips to quiet him.

"I have an idea," Haman's wife, Zeresh, said. "Let a gallows be made fifty cubits high, and tomorrow persuade the king to allow Mordecai to be hanged on it."

"Then," one of his friends said, "you can go into the banquet and truly enjoy yourself."

"You have solved my problems for me, Zeresh. Let the gallows be built, just as my wife has said," Haman barked this command to his servants.

"How can he do that?" Peter whispered. "Someone has got to stop him!"

"But how?" Matthew asked.

"I don't know, but there must be a way," Hiram

answered. "We have to get back and tell Katie and Ashtel what he is planning. Someone has to warn Mordecai. But first, I must deliver this letter to Haman. Wait for me around the corner. I will be right back."

When Hiram returned after only two or three minutes, the boys ran as fast as they could to deliver the terrible news of Haman's new plot to Ashtel and Katie.

Inside the palace, the boys ventured near the queen's chamber to see if they could find Katie and Ashtel. But all was quiet.

"No one is awake. I don't dare go any closer. We would be in trouble if we were caught here," Hiram whispered.

"Why don't we return in the morning? Nothing will be done before then anyway," Matthew reasoned.

"You are right," Hiram agreed. "Let us return to the king's chambers."

They walked through the dark palace halls, now lit only by moonlight, toward the king's quarters. The legions of archers carved in the stone walls seemed to march silently alongside them as they went.

"Hiram, thank goodness I found you!" One of the king's servants appeared suddenly out of the darkness. "Come quickly! The king cannot sleep and has asked for the book of the chronicles to be brought to him. Bring it to his chamber at once."

Matthew and Peter followed Hiram to a large room that contained hundreds of books and scrolls, upon which were written all the dealings of the kingdom. Hiram pulled a large volume from the shelf and hurried into the king's chamber to read to him. Matthew and Peter entered with Hiram,

but sat quietly just inside the entrance, so as not to disturb the king.

The king lay on his couch, restless and unable to sleep. When he saw Hiram, he said, "Ah, here you are. You may begin."

Hiram opened the book and began reading. He read of several recent occurrences in Shushan, and then began reading this: "'In those days, while Mordecai sat in the king's gate, two of the king's chamberlains, Bigthan and Teresh, of those which kept the door, were wroth, and sought to lay hand

on the king Ahasuerus. And the thing was known to Mordecai, who told it unto Esther the queen; and Esther certified the king thereof in Mordecai's name. And when inquisition was made of the matter, it was found out; therefore they were both hanged on a tree.'"

"Stop there," the king commanded. "Perhaps this is what has been troubling me: What honor and dignity hath been done to Mordecai for saving my life?"

"Nothing has been done for him, Your Majesty," Hiram answered.

"Nothing?"

"No, sire. I believe nothing has been done," Hiram repeated.

The king sat, deep in thought. "That must change. Mordecai must be bestowed with honor and dignity for his loyalty to me."

Chapter Nine

"Hang Him Thereon"

The next morning, Haman paced in the outer courtyard of the king's court, waiting to speak to the king about his plan to hang Mordecai from the gallows that had been prepared.

"Who is in the courtyard?" the king asked his attendants.

"Haman stands in the courtyard, Your Majesty," a servant answered.

"Let him come in," the king directed.

Haman came in and bowed low before the king. "Good morning, sire," he said in greeting.

"Good morning, Haman. Last night I was unable to sleep. My mind was filled with gratitude for one man—a man who has been loyal and true to me. I realized that I have not adequately recognized his service. Suppose I wanted to honor such a man? What, in your opinion, would be a fitting reward for such a noble man?"

Haman, his mind racing, lowered his head in false modesty. He thought to himself, *Who would the king want to honor more than me?*

"Well, sire," Haman answered with cunning. "If I really wanted to honor someone, I would have the king's own robe placed upon his shoulders, and the king's crown set on his head. I would command that the king's horse be brought for him to ride." At this point, Haman paused, giving the king time to consider his suggestions.

"Very good, go on," the king encouraged him.

"Well, all this could be delivered to the man by one of the king's noble princes. When the prince had dressed the man in the king's apparel, and sat him upon the king's horse, the prince would lead the horse through the streets of the city, proclaiming all that the man had done for the king," Haman declared, imagining himself riding the king's horse through the city, wrapped in the king's robe, the royal crown on his head.

"An excellent idea," the king readily agreed. And

then the king stood and commanded, "Haman, make haste and do all that you have said unto my servant, Mordecai. Thus it shall be, because he saved my life."

Haman was stunned. "As you wish, Your Majesty," he managed to mutter through his tightly clenched teeth. He bowed, concealing his rage from the king, and left to do as he had been commanded.

Being forced to parade the very man who had defied him so publicly through the streets of the city and to loudly declare his virtues was almost more than Haman could bear. He could feel the eyes of all the Jews on him as he showered honor upon Mordecai.

Hiram, Matthew, and Peter stood among the crowd near King's Gate, amazed by the spectacle before them. Only last night they had heard Haman's evil plot to hang Mordecai on the gallows! And now they watched as Haman led Mordecai through the streets of the city like royalty, with Mordecai perched on the king's horse, wearing the king's royal robes.

"Only God could perform such a miracle," Hiram whispered.

"Well, we're going to need one more to save all the Jews," Matthew reminded him.

"Well, if God can perform one amazing miracle, why not two? But how about you fast, and I'll pray," Peter suggested with a grin.

"Divide and conquer, huh?" Hiram responded with a wry smile. Then, "Come on, you two, let's go see if we can find out how Mordecai came to be honored by the king."

As they hustled through the courtyard in front of the king's quarters, they almost collided with the king's procession, making its way to the second banquet given by Esther.

"Haman doesn't look too happy," Peter observed as the king and his attendants passed by. Haman followed closely behind the king, his face pinched and angry.

At the door to the queen's chambers, the king's chamberlain gave three loud knocks on the door, announcing the king's arrival. The door swung open, and the king and Haman disappeared into the queen's dining hall.

Esther greeted her guests and seated them at the table, a sumptuous banquet laid before them once again.

From their positions behind Esther's lounging couch, Katie and Ashtel had a clear view of Haman and the king. Neither girl dared speak, but they exchanged furtive glances.

Esther nodded to a handmaid, who stepped forward to fill the golden goblets with sparkling red juice. The king swirled the liquid in his goblet, took a drink, and closed his eyes for a long moment. Then, opening his eyes again, he turned to Esther and repeated the question he had posed twice on the previous day.

"What is your petition, Queen Esther? It shall be granted you, even to the half of my kingdom."

"If I have found favor in thy sight, O king, . . . let my life be given me at my petition, and my people at my request," she asked simply. "For we are sold, I and my people, to be destroyed, to be slain, and to perish."

The king sat in stunned silence, bewildered by her request. "Who is he?" the king demanded

when he found his voice. "Where is he that dares presume in his heart to slay you and your people?"

"The adversary and enemy is the wicked Haman," Esther said softly.

The king stood up in a rage. He stormed angrily out of the room and into the palace garden.

Haman cowered on the other side of the table, his head in his hands, trembling in fear. Just yesterday, he was second only to the king in rank and stature. Today, the king was infuriated with him.

While the king paced wildly in the palace garden, Haman, desperate to save his life, threw himself on Esther and begged for mercy.

The king entered the room and saw Esther's servants dragging Haman away from the queen.

"Yes!" cried the king. "Take him away."

The servants covered Haman's head as one doomed for death and took him from the room.

Harbonah, one of the king's servants, approached the king and announced, "Did you know, sire, that on his property, Haman had a gallows made fifty cubits high on which to hang Mordecai?"

"He planned to hang Mordecai?" Katie whispered, shocked by the revelation.

"I wonder what the king will do now," Ashtel whispered in reply.

In an instant her question was answered, as the king roared his command: "Hang him thereon!" Then he ordered the servants out of the room. "Leave us!" he barked.

Ashtel and Katie hurried out with the other servants, leaving the angry king and his grateful queen all alone.

Chapter Ten

Hard Things Made Easy

"Come, let us find Hiram and your brothers," Ashtel said as she grabbed Katie's hand and dragged her across the maze of courtyards and hallways that led to King's Gate.

"There they are! Matthew, Peter, over here!" she waved to the boys, darting through the crowd to meet them.

"Have you heard the news?" Peter asked his sister.

"Oh yes, we've heard. We were there when Esther told the king it was Haman who plotted to kill the Jews," Katie said.

"Little did he know that Esther was a Jew," Ashtel added.

"You should have seen the king's face when he

realized what Haman had done. He was *so* mad!" Katie said.

"If Esther had not risked her own life, not only Mordecai, but all the Jews would have been killed," Matthew observed.

"Including us," Hiram said quietly, giving an impulsive hug to his sister.

"So much has happened! Was it really only yesterday that Esther went in unto the king?" Katie asked, shaking her head at how quickly everything had changed.

"You and I have been through a lot together, though we have been friends only for a short time," Ashtel said as she put her arm through Katie's. "It was wonderful to have a friend like you at my side through all of this," she added, her appreciation for Katie heartfelt and earnest.

"And I am glad to have a friend like you too. That is why it is going to be so hard to say goodbye," Katie said sadly.

"You're not going soon, are you?" Ashtel asked in dismay.

"I'm afraid we must. Our family is waiting for us to return," Matthew explained.

"Then you must promise to return someday," Ashtel insisted.

"As soon as is humanly possible," Katie promised, her blue eyes starting to tear up.

"Oh no!" Peter said, rolling his eyes. "Let's get going before you start to cry. I can't stand it when you cry."

Katie put on a brave face and hugged Ashtel tightly. "I'll never forget you and Queen Esther. Not ever!"

"And I will never forget you," Ashtel said tearfully.

Hiram shook Matthew's and Peter's hands warmly. "I hope you will return, but don't think we have this much excitement here all the time. Come, Ashtel, we have work to do before the day's end."

The children waved their good-byes as Ashtel and Hiram disappeared into the palace. Matthew led Katie and Peter to the spot where Mordecai had sat in defiance of Haman's order to bow. "I think this would be a good spot for our departure, don't you?"

"Then we'll always remember to be as brave and true as Mordecai," Peter said.

They took one last look at the magnificent Shushan Palace, locked hands, and felt their feet leave the ground. In barely a moment, they were deposited, breathless, on the soft pillows in Grandma's art cottage.

Grandma read on, seemingly oblivious to her three grandchildren trying to catch their breath. "'On that day, . . . Moredecai came before the king; for Esther had told what he was unto her [that she was his niece!]. And the king took off his ring, which he had taken from Haman, and gave it unto Mordecai. And Esther set Mordecai over the house of Haman.'"

"Well, that was one exciting story," Grandma said, setting her Bible on the table.

"If you think it was exciting *reading* about it, you should have been there in person!" Peter exclaimed.

"In person?" Grandma was puzzled.

"There you go again, Peter! Your imagination is always getting away from you," Matthew said, laughing it off and giving Peter a wink.

"I can't help it," Peter played along. "I was born with this imagination!"

"Well, don't ever change," Katie assured her little brother, "because we like you just the way you are."

"This is the time I always look forward to the most. I can't wait to hear what you have learned. Who wants to go first?" Grandma asked her grandchildren with great anticipation.

Peter answered first. "That king is a pretty powerful guy. You don't ever want to cross him, that's for sure."

"If I had to say what I learned," Katie began thoughtfully, "it would be what I learned from Esther."

"And what would that be?" Grandma asked, although she already had a pretty good idea.

"I never realized how much courage it took for Esther to go to the king and plead for the Jews," Katie said. "It could have easily cost her life. But Mordecai told her that if *she* didn't do it, the Lord would find someone else to accomplish His purposes."

"I felt just like Esther when I was called on a

mission," Grandma said thoughtfully. "I realized that if I didn't go and tell people about the gospel, Heavenly Father would find someone else to do His work. But maybe being a missionary was part of why *I* came to earth, so I did what God wanted me to do, and I have always been glad that I did. I didn't want to lose out on my destiny."

"Even though it was hard?" Katie asked, thinking about her own situation with her club.

"Yes, my dear granddaughter." Grandma looked warmly into Katie's eyes. "Even though it was hard."

"Here's something I learned," Matthew jumped in. "Mordecai also showed great strength in not bowing to Haman. It couldn't have been easy to be the only one sitting firm while everyone else around you was bowing."

"You could only do it if you knew you were doing what was right. When you know you're doing what's right, it makes doing hard things much easier," Peter spoke with authority.

Katie listened quietly to her younger brother, surprised by his wisdom. "I had no idea you were such a great thinker, Peter," she said.

"I pick up on a lot of things when you don't think I'm listening," he replied, with a shy smile.

"I've been doing some thinking myself," Katie said with determination in her voice. "When I came here today, I thought I had such a big problem. But when I think about Esther and what she faced, my problem doesn't seem so big anymore. Really, the worst that could happen to me is that I might get kicked out of the club. It's not like I'm going to die or anything."

"Let me get this straight." Matthew sounded impressed. "You're willing to talk to the club president even though she doesn't want Charlie at meetings anymore. Is that right?"

"That's right! I will do it!" Katie declared emphatically. "To quote a great thinker, 'When you know you're doing what's right, it makes doing hard things much easier,' right, Peter?" Katie reached over and gave Peter a hug, pulling him close to her.

"Okay, okay, that's enough!" Peter replied, squirming out of his sister's grasp. "You don't need to thank me anymore, Sis. I get it."

"Grandma, do you still have some of those Oreos left?" Katie asked. "I'm starving!"

"It's a good thing I hid a package, or your brothers might have eaten all of them," she teased.

"I bet I can find them before you do," Peter challenged Matthew, and he bolted for the cottage door.

"Oh, no, you don't," Matthew declared, and he took off after his brother.

That left Katie and Grandma to lock up the art cottage alone. On the way back to the house, Grandma asked, "Well, Katie, have you decided exactly what you're going to say to the president of your club?"

"Not exactly, but I'm going to follow Esther's example. I've decided to fast and pray about it first, and then I'm sure I'll know what to say," Katie said thoughtfully.

"No doubt about that, honey. Heavenly Father will help you. To paraphrase a great scripture, 'Who knows but that you joined the club for such a time as this?'" Grandma flung her arm over Katie's shoulder, and together they made their way back to the house.

About the Authors

Alice W. Johnson, a published author and composer, is a featured speaker for youth groups, adult firesides, and women's seminars. After receiving a B.A. in economics from Brigham Young University and serving a mission to Taiwan, Alice was an executive in a worldwide strategy consulting company, and then in a leadership training firm. She is now a homemaker living in Eagle, Idaho, with her husband, Paul, and their four young children.

Allison H. Warner gained her early experience living with her family in countries around the world. Returning to the United States as a young woman, she began her vocation as an actress and writer, developing and performing in such productions as *The Farley Family Reunion.* She and her husband, David, reside in Provo, Utah, where they are raising two active boys.

About the Illustrator

Casey Nelson grew up the oldest of eight children in a Navy family, so she moved quite often during her childhood. Graduating with a degree in illustration, she taught figure drawing in the illustration department at Brigham Young University, worked as an artist for video games, and performed in an improvisational comedy troupe. Casey is employed by the Walt Disney Company as a cinematic artist for their video games.